Homage

There,
      In the garden of heaven.

There,
      Where matter doesn't exist.

There,
      Where the spirit of beings is
pure.

There,
      you will live, my friend,
      In the peace of eternal light.

This book is dedicated to the memory of
Josep Cases i Cervera, 'Pepe'.

BRIEF HISTORY

The history of Barcelona is linked to the culture of the peoples of the Mediterranean Sea. Ever since the first settlements of Iberian tribes right though to the present day, the city's growth has been affected by cultural, political and social influences of all kinds, including the following:

Early 1st century
The founding of the Roman city.

Between the 1st and 4th centuries
The construction of the first city walls.

719
The Muslim invasion

985
The city is sacked by the Arab leader Al Mansor.

1249
First election of councillors.

1265
The Consell de Cent (Council of One Hundred) is formed.

1289
The founding of the Generalitat or the Diputació del General, a committee of 12 men representing the nobles, senior clergy and leading merchants and including three auditors.

End of the 13th century
Work begins on the second ring of city walls.

1367
The establishment of the court of the Maritime Consulate.

1359
Work begins on the third ring of city walls.

1373
The opening of the Saló del Consell de Cent.

1380
Building work begins on La Llotja (the commodities exchange)

1401
Founding of the Banc Municipal or exchange

1474
The first printing press arrives in the city.

1493
The Catholic Monarchs receive Christopher Columbus in Plaça del Rei

1519
Emperor Carlos I visits the city.

1527
The seawalls are built as a defence against pirates and privateers.

1610
Miguel de Cervantes visits the city.

1640
Peasant uprising known as the Reapers' War against the Spanish monarchy.

1652
Barcelona surrenders to Felipe IV, signalling the end of the Catalan Secession.

1704-1714
The War of the Spanish Succession.

1715
The city neighbourhood known as La Ribera is destroyed to make way for the military citadel.

1716
The Catalan political system is abolished.

1770
The second ring of city walls is knocked down and work begins on developing La Rambla.

1808-1814
Napoleon's troops invade the city.

1827-1852
Passeig de Gràcia and Passeig d'Isabel II are opened. The seawalls are demolished.

1835-1837
Excavation of the original Roman city begins.

1844
The first Teatre del Liceu opera house is built.
1848
The railway line between Barcelona and Mataró, the first in Spain, is opened.

1850
Electrical street lighting is introduced.

1859
Approval is given to Ildefons Cerdà's plan to build a suburban expansion area – the Eixample – based on a grid of streets that cross at right-angles.

1882
Work begins on La Sagrada Família

1888
The Universal Exhibition is held in Ciutadella Park.

1910
The rise of Modernisme in Catalonia.

1925
Plaça de Catalunya is developed.

1929-1930
The International Exhibition is held on Montjuïc.

1932
The Catalan Statute of Autonomy.

1936-1939
The Spanish Civil War.

1978
The Spanish Constitution is promulgated.

1979
Municipal elections and the forming of the first democratic city council.

1980
New Catalan Statute of Autonomy.

1992
The Olympic Games are held in Barcelona.

1995
Opening of the MACBA (Barcelona Museum of Contemporary Art).

1996
Thousandth anniversary of the founding of Catalonia.

1999
Opening of the new Teatre del Liceu and of the World Trade Center in Barcelona.

2000
Opening of the 1,150-metre long Porta d'Europa drawbridge in the Port Vell (old port).

Forum 2004.

BARCELONA

BARCELONA

Visiting the Cathedral

Opening hours: 9:00 a.m. — 1:30
4:00 p.m. — 7:00 p.m.

1. The chapel of Saint Christ of Lepanto.
2. Choir.
3. The Crypt of Saint Eulalia.
4. The High Altar.
5. Organ.
6. Lift to the roof.
7. The cloister.
8. Museum.
9. The chapel of Saint Lucia.

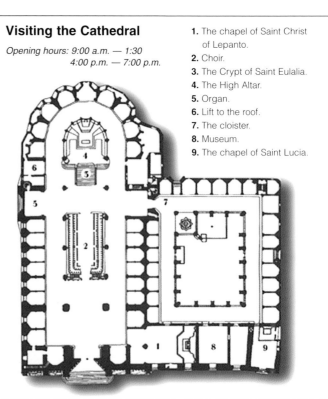

The Cathedral

The Cathedral of Barcelona is in the centre of the Gothic Quarter and is one of the finest examples of the Catalan Gothic style. Built between the end of the 13th century and the middle of the 15th century it is dedicated to Saint Eulalia, the copatron saint of the city.

On its present site there existed a 6th century Paleo-Christian basilica, destroyed by Al Mansor at the end of the 10th century. The Count of Barcelona, Ramón Berenguer, and his wife Almodis decided to build another cathedral on the ruins in Romanesque style, and this work was undertaken in the middle of the 11th century.

The present Cathedral is in Gothic style and consists of three naves with one apse and side chapels.

The places recommended for a visit are the Choir, the Crypt of Saint Eulalia, the Cathedral Treasury, the Cloister and the Museum.

The Choir is in the central part of the Cathedral and its decoration is of considerable artistic value. The stalls on the upper part are painted with the Coats of Arms of the knights who attended the Chapter of the Golden Fleece convened by Carlos I, and were made by Catalan and German craftsmen. The great Castilian sculptor Bartolomé Ordóñez made the entrances to the Choir, and was responsible for the

B A R C E L O N A

BARCELONA

decoration of the exterior facade of the choir.

The Crypt of Saint Eulalia. who was martyred in Barcelona in the 4th century. is under the High Altar. Relics of the saint are to be found inside the white marble sarcophagus

The tombs close to the High Altar are those of the Count of Barcelona, Ramón Berenguer, and his wife Almodis. Also near the High Altar is the Sacristy, through which the Cathedral Treasury is reached. Here are to be found art works of incalculable value

The Romanesque gate of San Severo leads from the inside of the Cathedral to the Cloister. In this peaceful enclosure with its palm trees and geese, you can see the fountain and the carving of "La Pietat" -"The Piety"- on the upper part of the door of the same name. Through the Cloister, access is gained to the Chapel of Saint Lucy and the Cathedral Museum where you can see "La Piedad", a work by Bartolomé Bermejo dating from the end of the 15th century.

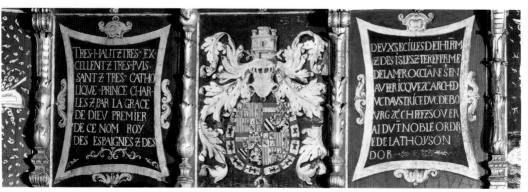

Plaça del Rei

One of Barcelona's loveliest and most peaceful spots is the Plaça del Rei (Square of the King).

Situated behind the Cathedral, it is made up of 14th and 16th century Catalan Gothic structures, making it one of the most picturesque areas of the Gothic Quarter.

This singularly beautiful, rectangular square was formerly the centre of the Palace of the Counts of Barcelona or the Palacio Real Mayor, which was built in the romanesque period and reconstructed in the 14th century by Pere III, the Ceremonious.

To the left of the square is the 16th century Palau del Lloctinent; the front part is the Tinell Hall dating from the middle of the 14th century; to the right is the Royal Chapel or Chapel of Saint Agatha in Catalan Gothic style dating from the 14th century. Almost closing the square, next to the Chapel of Saint Agatha, is the Clariana-Padellás mansion in 16th century Catalan Gothic style, through which we reach the City History Museum, the Royal Chapel and the Tinell Hall.

Overlooking this exquisite architectural view is the slender tower of King Martí, built in the 16th century, with five porticoed stories.

Palau de la Generalitat

The Palau de la Generalitat in the Plaça de Sant Jaume in the heart of the Gothic Quarter is one of Barcelona's most interesting monuments on account of its architectural and historical value.

The building was begun in the 14th century and subsequently enlarged. It has two main facades: one in the Carrer del Bisbe, dating from the 15th century, and the other in the Plaça de Sant Jaume, dating from the 17th century. Through the gate on the Carrer del Bisbe you reach a courtyard with a lovely Gothic staircase leading to the 16th century Chapel of Saint George. The Golden Hall, St. George's Hall and the Courtyard of the Orange Trees are the parts of the building most frequently visited.

Catalonia was one of the first regions in the world to have an established institution representing the people. This was "Les Corts Catalanes", precursor of the "Generalitat" of Catalonia. The region was governed by the king and Les Corts as early as the 13th century, the latter being composed of aristocrats, clergy and the common people. Their deliberations brought about the decisions that governed the community.

The "Generalitat", a self-governing body within the Spanish State, was founded in 1359 during the reign of Pere III, the Ceremonious, when the Corts de Cervera were held. This was the origin of the "Diputació Permanent de les Corts Catalanes", later known as the "Generalitat" of Catalonia.

After the defeat of Catalonia in the War of Spanish Succession against Felipe V, the "Generalitat", which had represented the interests of Catalonia for four centuries, was abolished by decree in 1714.

After the elections of April 12th, 1931, the "Generalitat" was reinstated four days later, its President being the Honourable Francesc Macià. With the approval of "l'Estatut" -the Statute- of Catalonia in 1932 and the parliamentary elections thereafter, self-government for the Catalans was instituted on November 20th, 1932. "The Generalitat of Catalonia will be made up of Parliament, the President of the Generalitat and the Executive Council" (Article 14 of the Statute of Catalonia, 1932).

The official state bulletin of April 8th, 1938 signed by General Franco revoked the Statute of Catalonia. In 1977 however, the provisional "Generalitat", which had been hitherto in exile, was re-established with Josep Tarradellas as President, and in 1979 the Statute was proclaimed.

This, together with the parliamentary elections of 1980, expressed the will for self-government of the Catalan people.

The seat of the Presidency of Catalonia is the Palau de la Generalitat and that of the Parliament is the arsenal building in the Ciutadella Park.

The City Hall

The Town Hall building is in the Plaça de Sant Jaume opposite the Palau de la Generalitat.

The Town Hall has a Gothic facade to the left of the main one, which is of greater artistic value than the neoclassical facade built in 1844. The central door of the neoclassical facade is flanked by the statues of Jaume I, the Conqueror, and Councillor Joan Fivaller, the first being the founder of the Town Hall and the second the defender of the city's privileges.

Inside the building, the Saló de Cent and the Saló de les Cròniques are outstanding on account of their artistic and historical value.

The Saló de Cent, built for the municipal councillors, was opened in 1373 and decorated and extended during the 17th and 19th Centuries. From the 15th to the 18th century the "Consell dels Cent" established the guide-lines for governing the city in this Hall. From here, we pass on to the Saló del Consell de la Vila, built in the 19th century and used by Queen María Cristina during the Universal Exhibition of 1888.

The Saló de les Cròniques is the result of extensions that were carried out for the 1929 exhibition, when it was beautifully decorated with mural paintings by Josep Maria Sert based on true deeds related by Muntaner concerning the warlike feats of the Almogàvers in the East, led by Roger de Flor, in the 14th century.

Barcelona obtained its municipal Charter in 1249 as a privilege from Jaume I, the Conqueror.

The Church of la Mercè

A church constructed in the 18th century which formed part of an old convent, the structure of the church is formed by a central aisle and side chapels. The interior is decorated in marble panelling and very elaborate, beautiful latticework. Particularly noteworthy is the carving of the Virgin from the 14th century. The Virgin of Mercy is the patron saint of Barcelona and according to the calendar of saints' days her feast day is the 24th of September. The city celebrates the feast day of its patron saint with traditional and folk cultural events.

Santa María del Mar Church

Santa María del Mar was built in the 14th century in the area of La Ribera which was inhabited by sailors, merchants, traders and people of the port. Several brotherhoods, together with the port workers, took part in the building of this church, which was completed in only half a century, thus causing the construction to be in the purest Catalan Gothic style.

The interior of the church comprises three high naves, one in the centre and two side naves, and a series of columns (situated at an unusual distance for this type of building) which hold up the roof, giving it an appearance of spaciousness.

There is a fine portal on the facade with an enormous rose-window above it, flanked by two slender octagonal bell towers which, together with the attractive well-placed windows, provide a delicate and harmonious architectural effect.

The Picasso Museum

The Picasso Museum occupies several Palaces on Carrer Montcada which used to be owned by merchants of the era, and exhibits a wide collection of the painter's works. When the museum extension is finally completed, it will occupy Palau Berenguer d'Aguilar, Casa del Baró de Castellet, Palau Meca, Casa Mauri and Casa Finestres.

Palau Berenguer is a 15th century Gothic building; Casa del Baró de Castellet is 18th century; Palau Meca is a Baroque structure built around a courtyard; Casa Mauri is 17th century, also Baroque, and Casa Finestres is older, dating from the 13th and 14th centuries.

The Picasso Museum was opened in 1963 and extended in 1970 with contributions from the painter's work. In the eighties his widow, Jacqueline Picasso, donated further works by the painter.

Today the museum exhibits various collections of paintings, ceramics and engravings by Picasso, arranged according to the painter's different periods.

Particularly noteworthy paintings are "Primera Comunión," "Ciencia y Caridad," "Los Desamparados" from his blue period, works from his cubist period and different versions of Las Meninas, by Velázquez.

With the extension to 10,628 m², including the five previously mentioned palaces, the museum offers a showcase welcome to over one million visitors each year. A meeting hall, cafeteria, nine galleries for temporary exhibitions, a multi-purpose area, it is a space of great architectural value and includes mediaeval remains.

The dimensions and illumination of the galleries are key elements in the circular route, so a clear, orderly itinerary can be followed. All the spaces have been adapted for use by the disabled.

These improvements place the Picasso Museum among the most important art centres in Europe, an open, modern centre promoting city culture.

B A R C E L O N A

Plaça de Catalunya

The Plaça de Catalunya is undoubtedly the most popular and most crowded square in the city. It is the heart and business centre of Barcelona, always filled with the continuous bustle of cars and pedestrians. It is situated within the area of the former 13th century city walls, with 19th century Barcelona spreading out beyond it in the form of the "Eixample", the urban expansion undertaken by the architect Cerdá.

Leading from this square are the following streets: the Ronda de la Universitat, the Ronda de Sant Pere (formerly the city walls), the Carrer Fontanella, the Passeig de Gràcia and the Rambles.

The square is decorated with two lovely fountains surrounded by gardens and attractive trees together with different sculptures, among them the "Goddess" by Clará.

Plaça de Catalunya is the starting point for a walk down Barcelona's most famous street: the Rambles.

The Rambles

The Rambles used to be the course of a river that brought the water from the mountains to the sea. At one side was the 13th century wall with four gates, the Porta de Santa Anna, the Porta Ferrisa, the Porta de la Boquería and the Porta

dels Ollers. Outside the city walls were fields and some convents. The name Rambla (dry river-bed) was given by the Arabs. It was covered over in the 18th century when the walls were demolished and building was begun.

The whole length of the Rambles from Plaça de Catalunya to the statue of Columbus is divided into five parts and, going down towards the Port, these are named as follows: Rambla de Canaletas, with its popular fountain of the same name; Rambla dels Estudis, with the 18th century baroque church of Bethlehem and the bird market; Rambla de Sant Josep characterized by the popular flower market and the large market of Sant Josep or la Boquería built in the middle of the 19th century; Rambla dels Caputxins with the famous Liceu Theatre and the Plaça Reial, an oasis filled with beer taverns, both dating from the middle of the 19th century; and finally the Rambla de Santa Mònica, with the Plaça del Teatre, the statue dedicated to the promoter of Catalan theatre.

Continuing in the direction of the port, on the left is the Wax Museum installed in a 19th century building and which was opened in 1973. At the end of the Rambles stands the monument in memory of Christopher Columbus.

The Opera House

On 30 January 1994, a fire destroyed the old, outstanding Theatre of the Liceu, whose origins and stage tradition dated back to 1847.

The reconstruction of the new theatre was supervised by the architect I. Solá Morales and its successful completion marked by the inauguration on 7 October 1999. The new theatre seats 2,334 persons.

The stage is a technological wonder and the architectural centrepiece of the building.

The Foyer and other new spaces under the main auditorium complement the beautiful installations of the new Theatre of the Liceu.

BARCELONA

Plaça Reial

Its structure is neoclassical and it was designed by Daniel Molina in 1844 and completed in 1848. It is rectangular in design with porticoed galleries on which several stories have been built, the lower ones being filled with beer taverns and shops. The centre part of the square is a sunny area with a lovely fountain surrounded by palm trees and lamps which were designed by the young Antoni Gaudí.

At one end of the porticoed galleries a street leads to the Carrer Ferran, built in 1826, which takes us to the Plaça de Sant Jaume.

B A R C E L O N A

B A R C E L O N A

Fòrum Barcelona 2004

The Royal Shipyards

At the and of the Rambla de Santa Mónica to the right is the majestic site of the Reials Drassanes -Royal Shipyards-, a medieval building for the construction of sea-going vessels.

Pere II began its construction in the 13th century and a century later Pere III, the Ceremonious, extended and completed the work. At that time there were eight large spacious naves whose roof was supported by slender arches giving it the capacity to construct as many as 30 galleons at the same time. The walls of the building were part of the third circle of walls which Barcelona once had, and of which the 15th century Santa Madrona Gate can still be seen.

The Royal Shipyards were later used by the Navy and were restored in the 20th century to house the City Maritime Museum.

The Maritime Museum

The permanent exhibition of the museum consists of different styles of ships, paintings, figureheads, navigation instruments and nautical charts, illustrating maritime evolution in Catalonia.

The exhibition of maritime Barcelona between 1750 and 1850 shows the development of maritime trade with peninsular and colonial markets.

The great sea adventure, conjuring the salty tang of its scenes and music, makes for an exhibition where the courage and bravery of seamen overcame the barrier between continents which the sea often represented.

The temporary exhibitions form part of on-going activities within the confines of these glorious grounds.

The Port

The end of the Rambles is marked by the statue dedicated to Christopher Columbus, who appears to be showing us the vast panorama of the port that welcomed him after he returned from America.

The city owes the great riches it acquired in the Middle Ages to this port, which made it one of the main banking institutions in Europe.

The loss of ships and goods from the 10th to the 12th century on account of insufficient protection afforded by the anchorage, however, led to the construction of an artificial port.

The initial work was undertaken in 1438 when King Alfonso V, the Magnanimous granted the Councillors of Barcelona permission to build a port which would facilitate the loading and unloading of merchandise. After that, the new port continued to grow in different stages. A committee for work on the port was established in 1869, and thus a new phase in its existence began. The extension of the breakwater on the eastern side, which in 1882 reached the floating dock, together with the construction of the western quay completed in 1874, formed a port free from the accumulation of sand.

The Old Port

The World Trade Centre Barcelona (WTCB), opened in 1999, completes the restoration of the Old Port on the south side. The Port holds the widest range of leisure activities in the city: the Maremagnum commercial centre, the Aquarium, the Imax cinema, the Port Vell Marina, the Nautical and Maritime clubs, the Catalan History Museum, and the Maritime Museum.

The Aquarium

The Barcelona Aquarium is the biggest in Europe and the most important one in the world on the subject of the Mediterranean. It was opened in September 1995. The main attraction of this enclosure is the sharks in the Oceanarium, which has a transparent tunnel 80 metres long making the visitor feel as if he is at the bottom of the sea.

The complex occupies a total area of 13,000 m^2 and holds 8,000 examples of 450 different species.

The Oceanarium measures 36 metres in diameter, five metres deep and holds more than 4.5 million litres of water, equivalent to three Olympic-size swimming-pools.

Imax-Port Vell

The IMAX, PORT VELL cinema, opened in 1995, contains three different large-format projection systems under one roof: IMAX, OMNIMAX and 3D. This technology is currently being used in over two hundred cinemas across the world.

The projector advances the film horizontally. The sound system uses digital technology, giving the spectator 27,000 watts distributed over six quadraphonic channels.

The three projection systems consist of FLAT IMAX, where the film is projected onto a flat screen 21 metres high. The OMNIMAX system, which is projected onto a hemispherical screen 30 metres in diameter, and IMAX 3D, where the film is projected onto a flat screen and viewed with special polarised glasses.

The Catalan History Museum

The museum offers an interactive itinerary through the history of Catalonia, ranging from prehistory to the modern day, and explained by objects and documents, historical recreations, and audio-visual and computer equipment.

The visit is chronologically organised into eight subject areas: the origins, the birth of a nation, the sea, the edge of the empire, the industrial revolution, steam, the development of electricity, and the decline and resurgence of Catalonia.

The museum offers educational and teaching material for groups, arranged visits, bookshop, bar-cafeteria and library.

B A R C E L O N A

The Citadel Park

Its site was formerly occupied by the district of La Ribera, so-called because it was on the sea-shore. This district was constructed between the 13th and 14th Centuries and was inhabited by fishermen, artisans and rich merchants.

Historical events obliged the attractive district of La Ribera to be almost completely demolished to enable the Citadel to be constructed in its place.

The oppressive policies of the Count and Duke of Olivares regarding Catalonia caused a massive rebellion against the monarch Felipe IV. On the death of Olivares, Felipe IV changed his policy regarding Catalonia. He promised to respect the rights and freedom of the Catalans and an agreement was made between the monarch and the Catalan people. This agreement entailed handing over the northern part of the region to France, so in 1659 Rosellon, Conflent, Vallespir and part of Cerdagne were

given to the French.

On his death, Felipe IV was succeeded by his son Charles II who died without descendants, thus bringing about the War of Spanish Succession (1701-1714) between the followers of the two claimants, Philip D'Anjou of the Bourbon dynasty and the Archduke Charles of the House of Austria.

Catalonia took the side of the House of Austria which, after the treaties of England and Holland (who were initially allies) with France, decided to withdraw its troops from Catalonia leaving it to the mercy of the French monarch Felipe V.

The Catalans, led by the Councillor Rafael de Casanovas and General

Antonio de Villarroel, organized the Catalan resistance which ended on September 11th, 1714 after a heroic defensive stand.

Felipe V then began to implement repressive measures abolishing the "Generalitat" and the "Consell de Cent" -the Council of the hundred, sworn citizens. The university too was closed and the use of the Catalan language prohibited.

This period of history, sad to recall for the people of Catalonia, culminated in the construction of the Citadel, a walled fortress in pentagonal shape, built on the orders of Felipe V between 1715 and 1718 with the purpose of controlling the city.

The district of La Ribera was thus ordered to be demolished and the inhabitants of which were transferred to the Barceloneta district.

During the 19th century, the Ciutadella was used as a prison. Later, due to the influence of General Prim, a decree was published for the demolition of the Citadel and only the Governor's Palace, the church and the Arsenal have been preserved.

After 1873 when the Citadel was destroyed, the area was made into a public park, which was later enlarged and improved with gardens and monuments for the setting of the 1888 Universal Exhibition.

Later, after uprisings at the beginning of the 20th century in Barcelona, there came the dictatorship of General Primo de Rivera in 1923, after which the Second Spanish Republic was proclaimed. Catalonia regained its former freedom and in 1932 the Parliament of Catalonia was installed in the former Arsenal of the Citadel which in previous times had been the symbol of the repression of Catalan rights and freedom.

The last session of this Parliament was held on October 1st, 1937 due to the onset of the Civil War.

Later, the present Catalan Parliament assembled once again in this historic building and its activities were inaugurated on April 15th, 1980.

BARCELONA

The Zoo

The history of the present Zoological Gardens of Barcelona began in 1892, when a large collection of animals was acquired by the Town Hall authorities to be kept in the Ciutadella Park. At the time of the Universal Exhibition in 1929 new sections were added, including the aquarium, and the number of animals was increased with private donations, among them a pair of camels presented to the zoo by King Alfonso XII.

During the Civil War, almost all the zoo was destroyed by continuous aerial bombardment to which Barcelona was subjected. In 1940 the Town Hall authorities took charge of the zoo, and in 1959 the Municipal Zoological Service was created, which resulted in better organization and the acquisition of many animals. The Zoo has a general selection of mammals, birds, an aquarium, an aviary, reptile house and collection of primates which, with the 14 hectares expanse of the zoo, have made the Barcelona Zoological Gardens into one of the most important in Europe.

B A R C E L O N A

The Parc de Mar

This area has brought about the recuperation of an important sector in Barcelona, the "Poble Nou", which was where Catalonian industry first took off during the final thirty-odd years of the last century. This sprawling area was occupied by numerous industrial depots and factories which had for many decades compelled Barcelona to live "with its back to the sea". The Parc de Mar area also has a considerable number of facilities which, ever since the Olympic Games ended, have served as amenities for the district. At the same time, special mention should be given to the construction of the Olympic Port which was destined to the sailing events.

B A R C E L O N A

Montjuïc Area

The urban transformation of this mountain began in 1908. The construction of the National Palace, the Spanish Village, the Trade Fair Precinct, the Mies Van der Rohe Pavilion, and the Stadium for the 1929 International Exposition, and completed with the installations for the 1992 XXV Olympiad.

The new Olympic Stadium, the construction of Palau Sant Jordi, the INEFC installations and the creation of the Olympic Gallery are the centres of attraction of this large public space called Montjuïc.

The National Palace houses the National Museum of Art of Catalonia (MNAC), which exhibits collections of Romanesque, Gothic, Renaissance and Baroque art.

The Archaeological Museum exhibits remains of the Greco-Roman colonisation in Empuries, together with Iberian and Visigoth remains. The Ethnological Museum has examples of pre-Colombian culture and of other exotic countries.

The Joan Miró Foundation, headquarters of the Centre of the Study of Contemporary Arts created by Joan Miró in 1971, was opened in 1975. The Military Museum is to be found on the mountain summit.

The Mirador del Alcalde gardens offer excellent panoramic views over the city and port.

B A R C E L O N A

The Illuminated Fountains

The Illuminated Fountain of Montjuïc is a wonderful show of water, music, light and colour which can be watched on warm summer evenings in Barcelona.

The fountain is the work of the Catalan engineer Carlos Buhigas, who built it as the crowning glory of the Universal Exhibition installation in 1929. It offers visitors a fascinating display of changing combinations of water and colour formations.

Built in an elliptical shape measuring 65 x 50 metres at the base, it has two concentric containers measuring 35 and 12 metres which rise up in the centre of the fountain. The water falls from the edge of these containers, the capacity of which is more than three million litres, in a cascade mixing different colours together.

Every second, 2,600 litres of water pass through some 3,600 pipes which work progressively to form different shapes and patterns with the aid of 180 motors providing 1,500 h.p. The fountain's 5,000 lamps need a supply of 1,500 kilowatts of electricity.

In the fairgrounds of 1929, there were in addition another eighty fountains, which disappeared at the end of the exhibition to give way to the Trade Fair area. The Magic Fountain was the most outstanding attraction of all and enhanced the avenue with more than a hundred illuminated obelisks

BARCELONA

MNAC

The National Museum of Art of Catalonia explains the history of Catalan Art through its collections from the first stirrings of the Romanesque to the mid 20th century.

As a National Museum, it is composed of various centres spread across several locations in Barcelona: the National Museum of Art of Catalonia, the Museum of Modern Art, the Numismatic Bureau, and the General Library of the History of Art.

The collection of Romanesque art is

composed of a series of murals unique in its class and other artistic creations, such as paintings on panels, carvings, monumental sculptures, silver and goldsmithing and enamel work.

The collection of Gothic art is made up of fundamentally Catalan works, and chronologically shows the political, social, economic and cultural development of the Catalan territory.

The collection of Renaissance Art contains origin works of European from the 16th, 17th and 18th centuries.

The Archaeological Museum and The Ethnological Museum

This museum exhibits pieces which signpost the different stages of the history of man, from the Palaeolithic Age to the Visigoths.

The various exhibits on show at the museum (mosaics, amphorae, sculptures, etc.), bring together the typical characteristics of each age.

The Ethnological Museum houses temporary exhibitions, and provides an ethnological background of Africa, Central America and some areas of Asia.

In addition to the pre-Colombian collections it also exhibits contemporary cultural works.

The Spanish Village

One of the places that is a must to visit in Montjuïc is undoubtedly the Pueblo Español -Spanish Village- of Barcelona.

This construction, which contains examples of Spanish architecture of many different periods and styles, was created for the 1929 International Exhibition in order to offer visitors an idea of Spain's architectural and crafts heritage in the different regions. The buildings in this village are common to those of any town in Spain-there is a church, town hall, central square, shops and craftsmen's workshops, all representing life in small, Spanish communities. There is also a Museum of Industries and Decorative Arts

The twenty streets and seven squares inside the enclosure contain palaces. mansions and shops, and along with the monastery outside, give one the impression of being in a real village

The entrance to the Spanish Village is the Puerta de San Vicente, an exact copy of the one in the city walls of Avila, in Castile. The Plaza Castellana, a square which is Castilian in design, leads to the arches of Sangüesa, (Navarra), then to the large main square, la Plaza Mayor, where we begin our tour of the Spanish Village.

Crafts at the Spanish Village

By returning to the origins of the Spanish Village, in a resumé of the architecture, crafts and culture of the people of Spain, its objective has been to foster craft workshops, open to the public, where each craftsman can pursue his trade within a crafts-oriented setting and grounds.

Since 1997, the Association of Active Craftsmen of the Spanish Village has promoted hand-made products, including painted clothing, glass, stained glass, ceramics, embroidery, stone carving, etc., and controlling quality and origin.

Currently the workshops and trades are over forty in number, and have been selected for their originality and uniqueness.

The post-graduate workshop of Massana school is to be found within the grounds.

BARCELONA

The Miró Foundation

The Joan Miró Foundation is a centre dedicated to the study and promotion of the artist's work, and to encourage contemporary art.

The building was opened to the public in 1975 and designed by the architect Josep Lluis Sert.

The spaces are arranged so that light is predominant throughout, using openings that let in natural daylight.

The content of the museum is composed of works donated by the family of the painter and Joan Prats.

Paintings on cloth, paper, wood and other materials, sculptures, textiles and drawings constitute the foundation's basic collection.

The foundation also presents temporary exhibitions of contemporary art, thereby promoting young artists. In addition, it offers educational activities for the young.

A library, bookshop and cafeteria-restaurant offer visitors further amenities to complete their trip.

The Olympic Areas

The different competitions in the Barcelona'92 Olympic Games were set out in four large Olympic areas in the city of Barcelona itself. These four areas were perfectly interconnected due to the new city ring roads and the good coverage of the city's public transport systems. These four Olympic areas made it possible to achieve a concentration of activities strengthening the feeling one gets in a city where a great event is taking place as they are all situated within a ten-kilometre radius and the travelling time between one and another is never in excess of twenty minutes. Besides this, their location avoided any crowding of sports teams and equipment in one spot and made it possible to enrich and recover certain less favoured areas for the city.

The four sections dedicated to "Barcelona'92" were: the "Montjuïc" area, the "Diagonal" area, the "Vall d'Hebron" Area and the "Parc de Mar" area.

B A R C E L O N A

The Montjuïc area:

This area was the most important centre during the 1992 Olympic Games in Barcelona. The area has a great tradition in sports activities (due to the large number of sports facilities), cultural activities (The "Grec" theatre, Mercat de les Flors, Miró Foundation, and numerous museums) and recreational activities (the "Spanish Town", Amusement park, amongst others). Particularly outstanding in this area is what came to be known as the "Olympic Ring", a sports complex that included the Olympic stadium which had been constructed in 1929 and whose original facade was preserved, which was used for the athletics

BARCELONA

B A R C E L O N A

competitions and for the Games' opening and closing ceremonies. Also in the Olympic Ring was the Sant Jordi Palace created by the Japanese architect Arata Isozaki with a capacity for 17,000 spectators, home of the gymnastics, handball and volleyball events. The third major installation in the Olympic Ring was the Picornell swimming pools, where all the swimming, diving and synchronized swimming events were held. Mention should also be made of the INEF pavilion, created by Ricardo Bofill, the current home of the Sports University which housed the wrestling matches during the Games.

BARCELONA

B A R C E L O N A

The Olympic Gallery

The Barcelona Olympic Foundation was set up in 1993 as private cultural body. Its purpose is to provide a realistic picture of the Barcelona Olympic Games, and to promote and research cultural, ethical and sporting values. It maintains a permanent exhibition and research centre giving an overall view of the Barcelona Olympic Games and their significance to the city.

The Barcelona Olympic Foundation has its headquarters at the Olympic Stadium of Montjuïc and occupies an area of 1,535 square metres for the pursuit of its activities.

The Olympic Gallery was opened on 25 July 1993, one year after the opening of the Olympic Games.

The Gallery has a permanent exhibition of the 1992 XXV Olympiad of Barcelona, divided into a permanent exhibition space and various subject areas offering information and a view of the project and its results.

Furthermore, the precinct contains an auditorium, projection room, video library, archives, reception, shop and administration offices.

Barcelona Football Club

24 September 1957, feast day of the Virgin of Mercy, patron saint of Barcelona, saw the inauguration of the New Field. In 1982, it was the venue of the XII World Cup Championship, and in 1992 the XXV Olympiad.

Diagonal Area

Amongst installations in an area already renowned for its private sports club facilities and university campuses (also with an important sports infrastructure of their own) is the outstanding "Camp Nou", Barcelona Football Club stadium, with a capacity for 120,000 spectators. Jointly with the Mini-Stadium and the Sarriá Stadium (the R.C.D. Español football grounds), it was the major setting of the football competitions in the Barcelona Olympic Games. These installations form the F.C. Barcelona sports complex (comprising the "Camp Nou", Mini-Stadium, Palaces 1 and 2 of the Blaugrana, and the Ice-rink) that housed the judo competitions, while the tennis and horse-riding competitions were held just a few metres away.

With 110,000 members, a stadium holding 120,000 spectators, and twelve sports sections, the Barcelona Football Club is one of the leading sporting institutions in Europe.

Barcelona Football Club, which was founded in 1899 by Hans Gamper (a summer tournament has been held in his name since 1966), is at the present time an institution paying homage to its members and to the more than thirty chairmen and thousands of sportsmen who have defended the Club's maroon and blue colours.

The F.C. Barcelona Museum displays a chronological history of this Centenary Club, one of the best in the world.

Vall d'Hebron Area

This area has benefited from its status as an Olympic Area because it has been equipped with sports facilities after the Games in accordance with a policy seeking to enhance this part of Barcelona city. This first started with the construction of the Municipal Velodrome, opened in 1984 and which then played host to the world track cycling championships. The Valle de Hebron Sports Palace, bracketed for holding the handball competitions, and the archery field completed this area which also housed the International Youth Camp set up in the "Hogares Mundet" facilities.

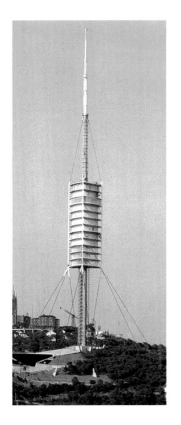

Tibidabo Mountain

Within the mountain range formed by the Catalan coastal chain, Tibidabo mountain is part of the Collserolas and, being almost 500 metres above sea-level, it is an ideal place for looking out over the 90 square kilometres of the city of Barcelona.

To get to the top of Tibidabo you can go by car via the Rabasada Road, or you can use another means of transport which is highly popular -the blue tramcar. The tramcar belongs to the Tibidabo Company founded in 1900 and its stop is at the end of the Calle Balmes.

On the mountain we also find the Fabra Astronomic Observatory built in 1904, and the Science Museum opened in 1981 thanks to the initiative of the cultural branch of the "Caixa", a banking concern with a long tradition in Catalonia.

B A R C E L O N A

BARCELONA

The Church of the Holy Family

The church has been under construction since Saint Joseph's Day (19th March) 1882.

The initial project was entrusted to the architect Francisco del Villar who began the construction of the crypt in neoclassical style. In 1883, Gaudí took over the direction of the work and when the crypt was finished, he changed the whole project, setting the seal of his own personal style in unmistakable fashion.

This church is intended to be symbolic of the church of Christ and its believers. The project consists of three monumental facades dedicated to the Birth, the Passion and the Glory of Christ. Each of these has four very high towers, which together symbolize the twelve Apostles. The great central spire symbolizes the Saviour and has four towers around it representing the four Evangelists. The apse has yet another fine spire representing the Virgin Mary.

The present state of the building process can be seen inside the enclosure. Here can also be found the model of the church, the crypt where Gaudí was buried, and the Museum dedicated to the architect's work containing plans, models and photographs of his other works.

BARCELONA

Antoni Gaudí

Born on 25 June 1852 to a boilermakers family, when Gaudí was 26 years old, he graduated as an architect and Eusebi Güell, his great hero, commissioned his first works as a professional. As a newcomer he designed the lampposts in the Plaza Real, later progressing to become the visionary genius of Modernista architecture.

Among his major works are: the Holy Family (1882 Villar, 1883 Gaudí); the Güell Palace (1885-1889), Casa Milá, "La Pedrera" (1905-1910), and Casa Batlló (1905-1907).

B A R C E L O N A

The Hospital of Santa Creu and Sant Pau

Designed in 1901 by Lluis Domènech i Muntaner and composed of a series of pavilions surrounded by gardens and interconnected by underground tunnels.

Its construction was made possible by the help of Pau Gil i Serra, a banker.

Nowadays one can freely walk through its gardens.

The Hospital of Santa Creu and Sant Pau is one of the founding works of Catalan Modernisme.

Güell Park

Commissioned by Count Güell, Gaudí designed this park as the location of a new urban development — a residential garden-city along the lines of the English model of the times. Although the project was not successful, today it is one of the most visited places in the city. The park was declared a UNESCO World Heritage Site for Humanity in 1984.

The entrance to the park is flanked by the lovely pavilions which emphasize the harmony of vegetation with stone.

The central staircase leads to the Hall of the Hundred Columns and is finely decorated with white

B A R C E L O N A

mosaic. A saurian head on the coat of arms of Catalonia decorates the central part, and further on, an enormous lizard is covered with pieces of polychromed mosaic.

The Hall known as the Cien Columnas -Hundred Columns- actually has 86 doric columns which hold up the great lookout terrace with its incredible undulating bench. Its mosaic and ceramic encrustations form a gigantic collage showing the impressive colour fantasies of Gaudí's work.

The main avenue in the park goes up the mountain-side solving the problems of the steepness of the land with viaducts made of local stone. The main avenues are wide and the terraces magnificent, with a vast lookout area. The groves of carob trees, olives, pines and palm trees, together with the Gaudí structures, make the Güell Park a complete urban achievement.

Finished in 1914, the park was acquired by the Town Hall Authorities of the city in 1922.

BARCELONA

Milá House

Casa Milá -Milá House- is popularly known by the name "La Pedrera" (the stone quarry) and is in Barcelona's most elegant street, the Passeig de Gràcia.

Its architect was Antoni Gaudí, who begun it in 1905 and completed it five years later.

The abstract nature of this construction appears to be inspired by the countryside surrounding Barcelona. Its shapes are in some way related to the elements around the city, namely the mountains and the sea. The plasticity of its external shapes express the rugged outlines of the Collserola mountains, and the undulations of the facade advance as if they were waves beating on the shores of the city.

BARCELONA

BARCELONA

Batlló House

Like "La Pedrera", the Batlló house is in the Passeig de Gràcia, and is also the work of Antoni Gaudí.

Begun in 1905, it took two years to build. It is also curious to note that next to the Batlló house are works by two of Gaudí's colleagues: Puig i Cadafalch and Domènech i Montaner.

The facade next to Batlló house belongs to Ametller house, the work of Puig i Cadafalch, and Lleó house is a little further down and is the work of Domènech i Montaner.

The three buildings were constructed during the first decade of the 20th century and represent the styles of the most characteristic architects of Catalan "Modernisme" or Art Nouveau.

↑

House Terrades "casa de las Punxes"
(Puig i Cadafalch)

← House Lleó Morera (Domènech i Montaner)

House Vicens (A. Gaudí)
↓

THE TAPIES FOUNDATION

The Tapies Foundation was created in 1984 by the painter himself with the aim of promoting the study of modern art. The museum holds a permanent collection of pictorial and sculptural works, drawings, engravings and lithographs contributed by Tapies himself in the course of his artistic career.

The building, classified as Modernista and the work of Lluís Domènech i Montaner, supports a sculpture by Tapies himself called "Cloud and Chair."

BARCELONA

BARCELONA

El Palau de la Música

The Palau de la Música Catalana is the work of Lluís Doménech i Montaner, the architect who built it in Art Nouveau style between 1905 and 1908.

The facade of the building is decorated with a sculpture symbolizing popular song. The inside reflects the prevailing Art Nouveau tendencies of the time, using mosaic, ceramic, and polychrome glass. The busts of Anselm Clavé and Beethoven symbolize popular Catalan song and universal music.

Opened in 1908, the hall is an artistic homage to Catalan Music and its most representative body, the choir L'Orfeó Català. The Palace was built to house this choir, and to provide it with concert halls.

The choir has its roots in popular songs, such as those of Anselm Clavé, and was founded in 1891 by Lluís Millet and Amadeu Vives. This was a time of creative rebirth, when the Catalan people were looking for their roots and a universal opening in social, political, economic and cultural spheres. In musical terms the spirit of the Orfeó is Catalan popular song and the interpretation of universal classical music, e.g., by composers such as Beethoven, Bach, Mozart, Wagner, etc.

The "Cant de la Senyera" by Maragall and Millet is still the collective symbol of this group at the service of

universal music.

The demolition of the church of Sant Francesc de Paula revealed the hidden facade and its redesign has given the building an entirely new look.

New halls and additional services will bring this master work of Catalan "Modernisme" fully into the 21st century.

The CCCB

The CCCB (Barcelona Centre of Contemporary Culture) occupies part of the Casa de la Caritat – a former poorhouse – next to the MACBA and the Cultural Studies and Research Centre. This building has been refurbished and has an attractive courtyard with unusual stuccoed decorative features and a glass wall inside. The CCCB works to promote contemporary culture by putting on exhibitions, courses in art and lectures and by studying major cities.

L'AUDITORI (The Auditorium)

The construction of this building, which opened in 1999 and was designed by the architect Rafael Moneo, was supported by the National Plan for Spanish Auditoriums. The Sala Simfònica (Symphonic Auditorium) has a capacity for an audience of 177, while the Sala Polivalent (Multipurpose Auditorium) holds 300 to 500. Both were designed to accommodate large symphonic orchestras as well as other kinds of performances. L'Auditori has a number of other facilities, including a press room, simultaneous translation, foyers for exhibitions and private study rooms, making it one of the leading centres for culture in the city.

The MACBA

The MACBA (Barcelona Museum of Contemporary Art), set in the residential district of El Raval, was designed by the architect Richard Maier and opened in 1995.

The works on display in the museum centre around its own collection of works dating from the second half of the 20th century based on three themes: the past, the present and the future. The permanent collection holds works by Spanish and international artists. The MACBA also holds temporary exhibitions, lectures and seminars as part of its work in culture and education.

The TNC

The Teatre Nacional de Catalunya (the TNC) was designed by Ricard Bofill's architects' practice and opened in 1997 under the founding director of Josep Maria Flotats. The theatre's three spaces – the lobby, the stages and the stage box – make up a single volume of some technical complexity. The Sala Gran (Large Auditorium) can seat 894, the Sala Petita (Small Auditorium) another 500, and the Sala de Tallers (Workshop Auditorium) a further 500. The theatre has a number of other facilities for the public, including a bar, restaurant and shops. The areas set aside for cultural activities include rehearsal rooms and a workshop for making sets. The TNC is owned by the Generalitat de Catalunya.

BARCELONA

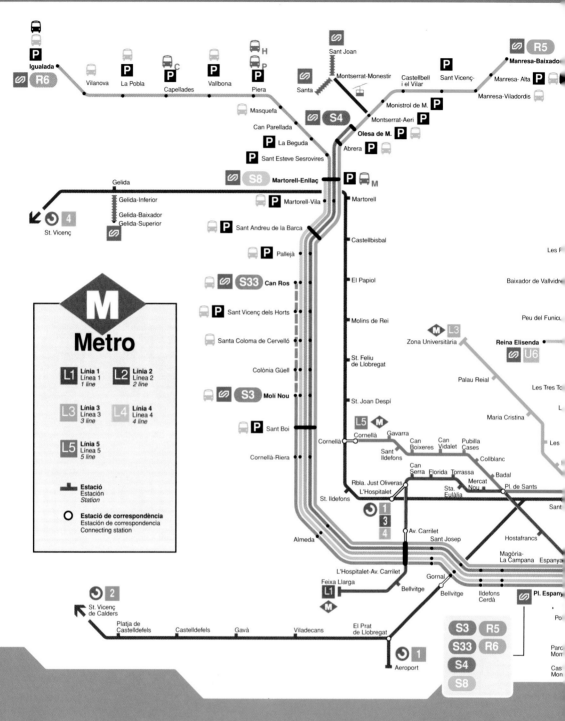

Igualada

R6

Vilanova La Pobla Capellades Vallbona Piera H

Santa Montserrat-Monestir Sant Joan

Masquefa S4 Castellbell i el Vilar Sant Vicenç- Manresa-Baixador R5

Can Parellada Monistrol de M. Manresa- Alta

La Beguda Montserrat-Aeri Manresa-Viladordis

Sant Esteve Sesrovires Olesa de M.

Gelida Abrera

Gelida-Inferior S8 Martorell-Enllaç M

Gelida-Baixador Martorell-Vila Martorell

Gelida-Superior

St. Vicenç 4 Sant Andreu de la Barca Castellbisbal

Pallejà El Papiol Les F

Baixador de Vallvidre

S33 Can Ros Molins de Rei Peu del Funicu

Sant Vicenç dels Horts

Santa Coloma de Cervelló St. Feliu de Llobregat Zona Universitària L3 Reina Elisenda U6

Colònia Güell Palau Reial

M Metro

L1	Línia 1 / Línea 1 / 1 line	L2	Línia 2 / Línea 2 / 2 line
L3	Línia 3 / Línea 3 / 3 line	L4	Línia 4 / Línea 4 / 4 line
L5	Línia 5 / Línea 5 / 5 line

Estació / Estación / Station

○ **Estació de correspondència** / Estación de correspondencia / Connecting station

S3 Molí Nou St. Joan Despí Maria Cristina Les Tres To

Cornellà L5 M Les

Cornellà-Riera Gavarra Can Boixeres Can Vidalet Pubilla Cases Collblanc Sant

Cornellà Sant Ildefons Can Serra Florida Torrassa Badal

Rbla. Just Oliveras Mercat Nou Pl. de Sants Hostafrancs

L'Hospitalet Sta. Eulàlia Magòria-La Campana Espanya

St. Ildefons 1 3 4 Sant Josep Almeda Av. Carrilet

2 St. Vicenç de Calders L'Hospitalet-Av. Carrilet Gornal Pl. Espany

Feixa Llarga L1 Bellvitge Bellvitge Ildefons Cerdà

Platja de Castelldefels Castelldefels Gavà Viladecans El Prat de Llobregat Pl. Espany

S3	R5
S33	R6
S4	
S8	

1 Aeroport

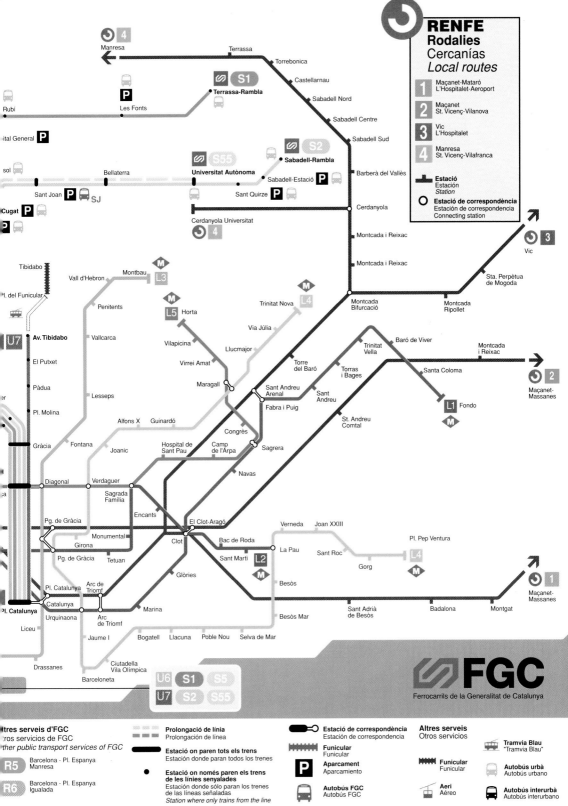

RENFE
Rodalies
Cercanías
Local routes

1	Maçanet-Mataró	L'Hospitalet-Aeroport
2	Maçanet	St. Vicenç-Vilanova
3	Vic	L'Hospitalet
4	Manresa	St. Vicenç-Vilafranca

Estació
Estación
Station

Estació de correspondència
Estación de correspondencia
Connecting station

Altres serveis d'FGC
Otros servicios de FGC
Other public transport services of FGC

R5 Barcelona - Pl. Espanya
Manresa

R6 Barcelona - Pl. Espanya
Igualada

Prolongació de línia
Prolongación de línea

Estació on paren tots els trens
Estación donde paran todos los trenes

Estació on només paren els trens de les línies senyalades
Estación donde sólo paran los trenes de las líneas señaladas
Station where only trains from the line

Estació de correspondència
Estación de correspondencia

Funicular
Funicular

Aparcament
Aparcamiento

Autobús FGC
Autobús FGC

Altres serveis
Otros servicios

Funicular
Funicular

Aeri
Aéreo

Tramvia Blau
"Tramvia Blau"

Autobús urbà
Autobús urbano

Autobús interurbà
Autobús interurbano

FGC
Ferrocarrils de la Generalitat de Catalunya

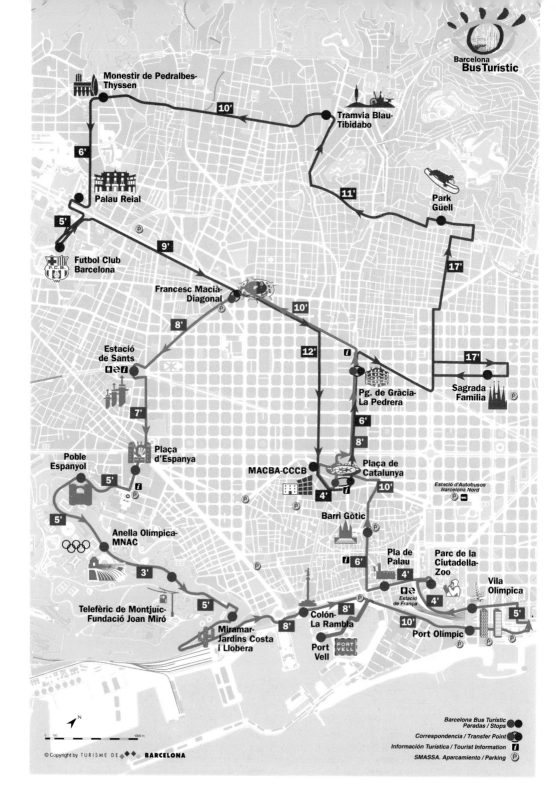

Barcelona
BusTurístic

Monestir de Pedralbes-
Thyssen

10'

Tramvia Blau-
Tibidabo

6'

11'

Park
Güell

Palau Reial

5'

9'

17'

**Futbol Club
Barcelona**

**Francesc Macià-
Diagonal**

10'

8'

12'

17'

Estació
de Sants

7'

Pg. de Gràcia-
La Pedrera

**Sagrada
Família**

6'

8'

Poble
Espanyol

Plaça
d'Espanya

5'

MACBA-CCCB

Plaça de
Catalunya

Estació d'Autobusos
Barcelona Nord

5'

4'

10'

Barri Gòtic

Anella Olímpica-
MNAC

3'

6'

Pla de
Palau

Parc de la
Ciutadella-
Zoo

4'

Vila
Olímpica

5'

Telefèric de Montjuïc-
Fundació Joan Miró

Estació
de França

4'

Colón-
La Rambla

8'

5'

8'

Miramar-
Jardins Costa
i Llobera

Port
Vell

**PORT
VELL**

10'

Port Olímpic

Barcelona Bus Turístic
Paradas / Stops

Correspondencia / Transfer Point

Información Turística / Tourist Information

SMASSA. Aparcamiento / Parking

N

0   100   1000 m

© Copyright by TURISME DE ◆◆◆ **BARCELONA**

PIRAMIDE EDITORIAL, S.L. Avda. Catedral, 3. 08002-Barcelona. Tel. 630 08 38 18. CIF: B17270869
Publishing director: Josep Cortés. Photographs: A. Argelich, A. Bofill, Calveras, Ll. Casals. R. Feliu, M. González, J. Llobet (Panorámicas), M. Llorens, R. Manent, R. Morera, R. Muro, M. Raurich, Sagrista, J. Sarrá, R. Solá, P. Virgili, Zerkowitz.
©Copyright by editor. All rights reserved. No part of this publication may be reproduced by any system, transmitted or otherwise copied for public or private use whithout prior written permission from the editor. ISBN: 84-89024-10-3. Printed in EU